# AFRICAN DRUMS

BY
BEVERLY
SCHMELZENBACH

BEACON HILL PRESS
OF KANSAS CITY

Copyright © 2015
by Beacon Hill Press of Kansas City

Printed in the United States of America

ISBN: 978-0-8341-3469-0

Cover Design: Keith Alexander
Illustrator: Keith Alexander
Interior Design: Sharon Page
Editor: William A. Rolfe

Author's Note: African Drums is based on a true incident. The missionary who 'spoke the language of the people', was my husband Harmon. He is the son and grandson of missionaries to Africa. Although the African boy, Makati, is fictitious, his life and actions depict the African culture. This All-reader children's book is part of the *Passport to Missions* curriculum for 2015-16.

10 9 8 7 6 5 4 3 2 1

# CONTENTS

# DEDICATION

Dedicated to my husband, Harmon, who showed me the Africa where he grew up and together we walked the trails of Africa.

# INTRODUCTION

African Drums is based on a true incident. The missionary who 'spoke the language of the people', was my husband Harmon. He is the son and grandson of missionaries to Africa. Although the African boy, Makati, is fictitious, his life and actions depict the African culture.

# 1
# MAKATI

Makati [Mah-KAH-tee] jerked awake and instantly sat up. His heart pounded as he strained to hear the noise again. He threw back his blanket, crawled off his sleeping mat and stood up. He was careful not to wake his young brother, Chibuto [Chee-BOO-toh]. As he cautiously opened the door a few inches, he heard the sound again.

His heart filled with dread as he peered out into the early morning light. *Just what I was afraid of,* he thought. He watched as four large drums were rolled out and placed at the base of an immense wild fig tree. The drums were carved from large stumps of wood and covered with bright red and yellow designs.

Makati knew it would be a long day of the Ngoma [n-GOH-mah]. Ngoma or witch doctor ceremonies are a day with special ceremonies worshipping the ancestors. There would not be a break in the wild hypnotic rhythm of the African drums. He feared the dark, haunting atmosphere that crowded these days.

Makati pushed the door open and went outside. The huge open courtyard was encircled with twelve round mud huts of all sizes. Slowly the village came alive with activity. His father stepped from his doorway. Tall and proud, he was the Induna [in-DEW-nah], the headman of this large village.

As Makati looked across the courtyard, he heard the first sound of a drum. He watched as two drummers' hands began to beat out a rhythm.

The sun had just appeared over the top of a thorn tree when Makati heard the rumble of a car approaching. Soon it appeared on the road, dust billowing behind it. He stepped close to his father and excitedly said, "That's the missionary's car, Father!"

It had been over a year ago when Makati had watched a green pickup go by. It was loaded with lumber and cement. Week after week, as he herded his father's goats a short distance from the church, he watched the walls slowly go up. Finally

a bright blue roof was hammered into place. Out in front of the church a sign read, 'Lebantla La MoNazareta' - 'Church of the Nazarene'.

Now, as he stood outside his father's hut, he heard a second car approaching. "Here comes another car!" he exclaimed. "They must be going to have a big celebration at the church." He wished he could go see what was happening but his father had forbidden him to go into the church.

Small groups of people began to arrive from the nearby villages. Grass mats were brought out and scattered on the ground for people to sit on. Some of the older men settled down on hand-made wooden stools. Soon the village was crowded with people and filled with noise as they talked and laughed.

Suddenly there was a disturbance at the main entrance. Makati stared as the old witch doctor, Sangoma [Sah-n-GOH-mah], entered. He had seen her before. She claimed to be able to speak with the dead ancestors. Everyone knew and feared her.

# 2
# SANGOMA

Makati slumped back as Sangoma walked just a few feet in front of him. He could smell the strong odor of stale animal fat from the raggedy skins that hung around her waist. A string of dried gourds filled with pebbles, was tied around each ankle and rattled as she shuffled along. Her hair was packed with greasy red mud and hung in short curly ringlets. She carried a switch made of wildebeest tails, tied together with strings of brightly colored beads. It was a symbol of her authority.

Three young men followed Sangoma, trudging into the center of the village. They were dressed like the old witch doctor. The people sat quietly and bowed respectfully as they passed by. Sangoma made her way to where the drums pounded their monotonous rhythm. She slumped her heavy body onto a grass mat in front of a nearby hut.

Makati's father was talking with his uncle. His father said, "Today is the graduation ceremony for the young witch doctors. They have worked long and hard for this day and will demonstrate their powers. This is a great day!"

Makati watched as the three young trainees began to dance in a circle to the beat of the drums. Dust filled the air as they danced faster and faster. The people clapped their hands, whistled and chanted.

Makati's watched as one of the trainees suddenly stopped and walked over to a hut. He reached up and probed the thatch roof. He pulled out a coin that had been hidden there. In triumph he lifted the coin and showed it to the crowd. Then he skipped over to the old witch doctor and gave her the coin.

"He's demonstrating his power," Makati's father whispered.

Immediately the young witch doctor returned to dancing and chanting. Then another trainee left the dancing group and crouched before Makati's white-haired grandfather. He reached up and took a coin from the old man's headband. The people laughed and clapped in approval.

The third trainee stopped, knelt down and dug in the cold ashes of the night's fire. He pulled out a coin and held it up to show the people.

Each time a coin was found, the young witch doctor presented it to old Sangoma. She accepted the gifts and silently nodded to the students.

Hour after hour the wild rhythm of the drums throbbed on and on. The new young witch doctors continued to demonstrate their powers.

The sun had passed far overhead when Makati saw the missionaries' cars returning from the church. He was surprised when he saw one car slow down and come to a stop on the roadway. The second car slowed then disappeared down the road. Makati watched the car doors open and the missionaries climb out. They hesitated a moment, then slowly walked along the footpath towards the village. They stood at the outside edge of the village. After a moment, one missionary entered the village and walked to Makati's father. Makati was amazed when he heard the missionary speak fluently in his own language. It was a difficult language with many clicks. Makati had been told that no white person could speak his African language.

# 3
# THE MISSIONARY

The missionary held out his hand and politely greeted Makati's father.

"Sawubona [saw-oo-BOH-naw] (Hello)," he said. "We are glad to see you."

Makati's father answered, "We see you and greet you."

They talked for a short while, the missionary said, "My friends would like to take some pictures, if we have your permission."

"You are welcome to take pictures," Makati's father answered.

The missionary thanked him and returned to join the other missionaries. They observed the entire village and intently watched the old witch doctor and the dancing trainees. Now and then they whispered to one another and silently took pictures.

Then Makati saw a strange thing. Three of the missionaries bowed their heads and closed their eyes. They stood silently for a few minutes then lifted their heads and once again watched the dancers. Then two others bowed their heads.

Gradually the beating of the drums slowed down and the rhythm changed. One trainee came close to Makati, kicking up the dust with his lively dancing. He was saying, "Why is it so hard for us to work today? O spirits help us to overcome the power that opposes us. Why are we being defeated?" He repeated it over and over.

Makati's dog slept at his feet. Suddenly it gave a low growl and jumped up. It darted over to one young witch doctor and bit him on the ankle. The witch doctor let out an angry yell and kicked at the dog. The dog slouched back. "Stay," Makati ordered.

Once again the drums slowed down. The old witch doctor, Sangoma, motioned for a different drummer to come. The new drummer began a frenzied beating on the drums. But there was no rhythm to his frantic pounding.

Sangoma struggled to her feet and walked over to the drummers. She motioned for one to move over, as she began beating the drums. On and on

she pounded, but failed to build up the rhythm. Soon she gave up and motioned the drummers to continue. She shuffled back and dropped onto her mat. A deep frown creased her dark face.

The young witch doctors searched and searched, but could no longer find the hidden coins.

All at once the leg rattle came loose from one trainee and dropped to the ground. He stopped dancing and looked over to old Sangoma. The dancing stopped while he reached down and tied the rattle back onto his leg. Makati heard him chant, "O spirits, why, are we having trouble? Who are these white people who are defeating us?"

On and on the drummers pounded furiously and tried to pick up the tempo. The people clapped their hands and chanted and whistled.

Many times Makati looked at the missionaries. Often he saw one or two with their heads bowed. They were no longer taking pictures.

As one trainee made a high jump, he came down on his ankle and twisted it. He limped away and sat in the shade.

"Look!" Makati whispered, as a wig fell off one trainee and the sash and bead belt of another came loose and fell to the ground.

# 4
# TROUBLE

"Father, what is happening?" Makati asked.

"I do not know. We have never had these problems before," he answered.

Makati watched as Sangoma rose and shuffled over to stand behind the young witch doctors. She started chanting, "Help us, O spirits! May the age old customs of our people overcome the power of these people opposing us today. I can find no opening in their defense. I see only darkness."

Sangoma stopped her chanting and walked over to the drummers. She raised her hand and told them to stop playing.

The drums were silent.

Sangoma motioned the witch doctors to follow her into the empty hut. It was not long before they all came outside.

Fear froze Makati as he watched his father walk over to the witch doctors. While they talked together, they kept glancing at the missionaries.

Makati's father left the group of witch doctors and walked over to the missionaries. He said, "You may leave now. The Ngoma is over. We cannot continue while you are here."

"Yes. We understand. We will leave now," said the missionary who spoke their language.

Makati's father politely asked, "Is there anything you would like to say to the people?"

The missionary stepped forward. In a strong voice he said, "We thank you very much for allowing us to be here today." He held up a small black book and said, "The Word of God says, 'For Unkhulunkhulu [Ewn-kew-lew-NKEW-lew] (God) so loved the world that he gave his one and only Son, that whoever believes in Him shall not perish but have eternal life.' We see that you are living in great fear and bondage. There is one who can set you free from the darkness that brings the fear of the ancestors. His name is Jesus. He can forgive your sins and fill your life with peace and bring you joy each day. May the God of heaven be with you."

The people listened intently while the missionary spoke. At the close of his short message, the missionary raised his hand in farewell. The missionaries turned and quietly filed back to their car and drove away.

Makati stared at Sangoma. She had a puzzled look on her face as she watched the car disappear. Then she seemed to jerk and with a startled look on her face, she called loudly, "We leave now!" The wild celebration had ended.

The young witch doctors followed Sangoma as she plodded out of the village. Slowly the people rose and silently left the village, following the footpaths back to their homes.

Makati inched his way close to where his father was seated under a thorn tree. Four of the tribal elders sat with him.

"This has not happened before," Makati's father said. "We have never seen Sangoma unable to continue the ceremony."

"Did anyone watch the missionaries?" asked an old man named Kala [KAH-lah].

"They were only taking pictures," Makati's father answered.

"I saw two of them put their heads down and close their eyes. What were they doing?" The elders could not seem to find an answer to the strange happenings of this day.

"Maybe they were talking to their God. I have heard they have a strange God. They don't fear their ancestors," said Govu [GOH-voo] another old man of the village.

"Their God must have great power to stop the Ngoma," said Makati's father.

# 5
# PERMISSION

That evening Makati approached his father.

"Yes son. You wish to speak with me?"

Hesitantly Makati said, "Father, I wish to go to the church and see what they talk about."

"No," Makati's father replied. "It is not good. We have our own customs and traditions. We do not need the white man's religion."

Respectfully Makati said, "Father, I want to learn what caused the witch doctor's ceremony to fail. Please consider it, Father."

Makati's father looked away for a moment. "I will think about it."

Six days later, once again Makati approached his father. "Have you made a decision, Father?" he asked.

"Yes," he answered. "I have spoken with the elders. You may go to see what you can learn. Take Chibuto with you to watch the goats."

"Thank you, Father." Makati respectfully backed away and then darted across the yard to tell Chibuto.

Early Sunday morning Makati and Chibuto herded the goats out of the enclosure and headed across the open grassland towards the church. The sun was half way up in the sky when the church came into sight.

They watched the people come from all directions and enter the church. Soon they heard joyful singing.

"Keep the goats here," Makati told Chibuto. "I'm going to go into the church." He hurried to the open door and quietly slipped inside. He sat down at the back on a rough wooden bench.

After a while the singing stopped and the pastor stood and walked to the front. He was dressed in the same kind of clothing the missionaries wore. He carried a large black book and read the same words the missionary had spoken.

Makati listened carefully. The preacher was talking about Unkhulunkhulu (God) and his Son,

Jesus. Then the pastor said, "Let us pray." Makati watched as all the people bowed their heads and closed their eyes. They were doing the same as the missionaries had done at the witch doctor ceremony. It sounded like the pastor was talking to Unkhulunkhulu.

Makati stood and quietly left the church. He ran towards Chibuto and together with the goats, they headed home.

When they entered their village, Makati's father was waiting for him. "Let us sit here," he said, as he pointed to two stools. "What did you learn, Makati?"

Makati tried to explain what he had heard. Then he gathered his courage and said, "Maybe next Sunday, I could learn more."

"Yes. Go again and learn more," his father replied.

The next Sunday Makati once again sat at the back of the church. He listened carefully to all that Pastor Mnisi [M-nee-SEE] said. But he still had many questions that needed answers.

# 6
# MEETING JESUS

On Friday Makati herded the goats towards the church. He came near to where a teenage boy was also herding a few goats. They greeted each other with the traditional greeting, "Sawubona."

"I am Makati."

"Hello, Makati. I am Samuel. I have seen you at our church. I am the son of Pastor Mnisi."

"Oh! I am happy to know you. I have many questions about the indaba [in-DAH-bah] (matter) that your father has spoken about," Makati said. They sat down in the shade of a thorn tree.

"Your father said that Unkulunkulu had a son that He sent to earth. Where is that son?" Makati asked.

"He lived on earth a long time ago—over 2,000 years ago."

"Who was his mother?" Makati asked.

"His mother's name was Mary. She was a young maiden who had never married. We celebrate Jesus coming to earth at Christmas time. Do you know about Christmas?"

"I've heard the word - Christmas. It is a time of gift giving. Where was this Jesus born and where did he live?" Makati asked.

"He was born in a town called Bethlehem and he grew up in the country of Israel. It is way far north of here. My father could tell you more than I can."

"My father is letting me come to your church. He wants to know how the missionaries stopped the witch doctor's ceremony." Makati told Samuel what had happened at the Ngoma three weeks before.

The next Sunday Makati listened carefully to Pastor Mnisi. He told how Jesus died and came alive again to bring forgiveness of sins and take away the fear of the ancestors.

Pastor Mnisi asked if anyone wanted to come forward and kneel at the altar and ask Jesus to forgive them and become their Savior.

Makati wanted to know this Jesus, God's son. He watched as a man and woman walked to the front and knelt down. Makati hurried forward and knelt down. Pastor Mnisi knelt by him and quietly prayed.

Makati prayed, "Hello, Jesus. It is me, Makati. I have never talked to you before. I believe you are God's son and the Savior of the world. Please forgive my sins and make my heart free of fear." Makati felt as if a heavy weight had been lifted from him. He wanted to sing and laugh. He had never felt like this before.

Pastor Mnisi said, "Makati, you are now a Christian. I will pray for you and your whole village. If your father is willing, I would like to come and talk to your people from God's word and tell them about Jesus."

"I will ask my father," Makati said. "Thank you. I want to learn more about the powerful God who was strong enough to stop the witch doctor's ceremony."

As Makati walked toward Chibuto and the goats, he prayed. "Dear Jesus, please help me to have the right words to say to my father. I want my village to become Christians and not fear the ancestors. Thank you for coming into my heart today."

# DISCUSSION QUESTIONS

**1.** Where did Makati's father forbid him to go? Why didn't he want Makati to go there?

**2.** What group of people showed up during the Ngoma or witch doctor ceremonies?

**3.** God answered the prayers of the missionaries during the witch doctors ceremony. Has God ever answered your prayers? Name one way God answered your prayer?

**4.** Makati's father told the missionaries they could leave. What did he allow them to do before they left?

**5.** Where did Makati's father finally allow him to go? Why did Makati's father allow him to go there?

**6.** What happened at the church that changed Makati's life? How has God made a difference in your life?